I'm OK Being Me

Activities to Promote
Self-acceptance and
Self-esteem in Young People
aged 12 to 18

Anne Betts

P·C·P
Paul Chapman
Publishing

Lucky Duck is more than a publishing house and training agency. George Robinson and Barbara Maines founded the company in the 1980s when they worked together as a head and as a psychologist, developing innovative strategies to support challenging students.

They have an international reputation for their work on bullying, self-esteem, emotional literacy and many other subjects of interest to the world of education.

George and Barbara have set up a regular news-spot on the website at

http://www.luckyduck.co.uk/newsAndEvents/viewNewsItems
and information about their training programmes can be found at www.insetdays.com

More details about Lucky Duck can be found at http://www.luckyduck.co.uk

Visit the website for all our latest publications in our specialist topics

- Emotional Literacy
- Self-esteem
- Bullying
- Positive Behaviour Management
- Circle Time
- Anger Management
- Asperger's Syndrome
- Eating Disorders

ISBN: 1-4129-1077-3

Published by Lucky Duck
Paul Chapman Publishing
A SAGE Publications Company
1 Oliver's Yard
55 City Road
London EC1Y 1SP

SAGE Publications, Inc.
2455 Teller Road
Thousand Oaks, California 91320

SAGE Publications India Pvt Ltd
B-42, Panchsheel Enclave
Post Box 4109
New Delhi 110 017

www.luckyduck.co.uk

Commissioning Editor: Barbara Maines
Editorial Team: Mel Maines, Sarah Lynch, Wendy Ogden
Illustrator: Philippa Drakeford, Simon Smith
Designer: Helen Weller

Printed and bound by The Cromwell Press, Trowbridge, Wiltshire

Oh child of today

Oh child of today
who is parent of tomorrow
come let's join hands and together we can walk
equal and respectful of each other.
Let us learn together
and build for ourselves and others a better future.

Oh child of today
who is teacher now in bud
come listen to our hearts and together we can feel
happy and sad for each other.
Let us share together
and build for ourselves and others a kinder future.

Oh child of today
who is our tomorrow
rise up and be yourself that we may see you clearly,
celebrating your uniqueness.
Be proud of who you are
and be for yourself and for others
an individual of the future.

Dedicated to children and young people everywhere.

Anne Betts, 1995.

Acknowledgements

My thanks and my love to my husband and children, Barry, Jo and Anthony for being okay with 'me'.

Graham Clayton (deceased) and Sylvia MacNamara my M.A. tutor; both of whom inspired and encouraged me.

Finally, to all the young people and adults who have agreed to take part in the programmes to measure self-esteem over the past twenty years.

How to use the CD-ROM

The CD-ROM contains a PDF file labelled 'Worksheets.pdf' which contains worksheets for each session in this resource. You will need Acrobat Reader version 3 or higher to view and print these pages.

The document is set up to print to A4 but you can enlarge the pages to A3 by increasing the output percentage at the point of printing using the page set-up settings for your printer.

To photocopy the worksheets directly from this book, set your photocopier to enlarge by 125% and align the edge of the page to be copied against the leading edge of the copier glass (usually indicated by an arrow).

Contents

Hierarchy of Needs Pyramid

Self-fulfilment

Self-esteem and achievement

Relationships

Safety and security

Basic physical needs

Foreword

Maslow (1968) drew his famous Hierarchy of Needs Pyramid in the late 1960s. It is often depicted as a pyramid consisting of five levels. The basic idea of this hierarchy is that higher needs come into focus only after all needs lower in the pyramid are met. This is a useful model for adults who hope to encourage achievement and motivation in young people. If they are not safe and secure, if their relationships are troubled, then they will be unlikely to reach their full potential. The adapted model was developed by Anne Betts over the years.

Anne Betts has used *B/G Steem* to demonstrate the success of her group work programmes. She has developed innovative and creative activities to raise the self-esteem of the young people she works with. It is to her credit that she has evaluated her work with vigour and published the ideas for others to use.

Barbara Maines and George Robinson

Introduction and Background

This book aims to support professionals working with young people who demonstrate behaviours common in those with low self-esteem. The DfES outlined proposals for long-term reform of the curriculum and qualifications for 14 to 19 year olds. These proposals from Tomlinson (February 2004) are focused on design features for a clear system for young people. One of the summary statements recognises, "failure consistently to equip young people of all abilities with the generic skills, knowledge and personal attributes they will need for future learning, employment and adult life".

It is my belief that young people need a feel-good factor based on self-belief if they are to engage in the process required to gain the generic skills referred to above. Often the opportunities are restricted by a curriculum and timetable akin to a straitjacket. This leads to a feeling of insecurity because there are no realistic choices. This in turn leads initially to an inability to make choices and eventually, a diminished self-esteem. "Healthy, positive self-esteem is a result of feeling secure and having self-respect, feeling confident to deal with life challenges," (Harvey 2000).

I have used the exercises and techniques outlined with an integral group and found that those with low self-esteem aspire to higher levels of achievement encouraged by their peers. Following fifteen years' research and practical analysis I hope that the supporting evidence and the framework of techniques and activities will enable the facilitator and learner to find strategies to develop the confidence and the skills required to lead a full life.

I believe that each person is a unique individual and has the right to be respected for that uniqueness. I recognise that some behaviours are not easy to respect but maintain that the person behind the behaviour still deserves that respect. All of the activities and exercises within this book have been developed with the learner. It is my aim that they provide opportunities for the learner to feel a sense of achievement and gain respect for and from self and others.

What is self-esteem?

Nelson-Jones (1993) describes a systematic people-centred approach in managing immediate problems. Plutchik (1962) discusses the importance of recognising inner emotions if one is to develop and reach one's full potential. Individuals who exhibit low self-esteem have usually found some difficulty in recognising and dealing with inner emotions. The result is that they learn 'problematic skills' – that is they learn to be very good at being bad. Social pressures and, in particular, peer pressures have been found to be contributory factors in reinforcing either positive or negative self-esteem that have resulted in behaviours unacceptable to schools, colleges and ultimately society.

Biggs (1978) discusses a mediational model of learning and study processes and suggests that independent variables exist prior to and independently of any single performance. The model further suggests that young people who are placed within an existing learning structure, for whatever reason, will be motivated to learn a particular task.

My research over the years would only partially support this opinion. I have found that just as a learner can be motivated by an approach that begins with their knowledge base, recognising and respecting that level of understanding, so can they be demotivated by a method with a rigid framework of aims that are to be taught. The demotivation of the young person then results in a feeling of separateness and failure with resulting low self-esteem. In either event this is due to individual differences, but the two main dimensions of performance:

- quantitative (how much has been learned)
- qualitative (how it has or hasn't been learned)

are not easily identified if a young person is not motivated. I would extend the model offered by Biggs and Kirby (1984) to take into account all external and internal factors to an individual. I summarise my model as follows:

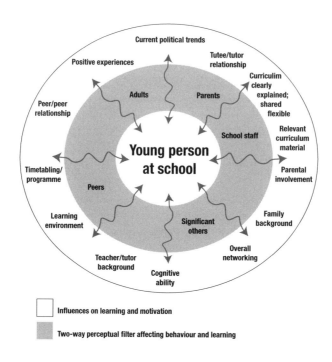

Different things, people, places, rewards and punishments have an effect on how people act. A person who is internally motivated is usually self-motivated and knows what their goal is, how to get there and will achieve that goal to varying degrees. Other people may be motivated by external factors such as money or finishing class or work early. This person is usually compliant with a goal identified by others with punishment as an outcome for lapses into inactivity or non-achievement. A person with high self-esteem who is internally motivated can be 'labelled' as headstrong or difficult and may be indifferent to rewards or sanctions. Unfortunately it is my experience that some of these individuals display inappropriate behaviours and when excluded from mainstream society lapse into petty crime or anti-social activities. Those with low self-esteem who are externally motivated on the other hand may become immune to punishments and failing becomes the norm for them.

Maines and Robinson (1988) developed a measure to help identify low self-esteem and locus of control. Their aim was to investigate the influence of self-concept on children's learning and behaviour and consider the possible association between self-concept and whether they were internally or externally motivated.

In 1989 while working as a volunteer I used this measure with a group of young people alongside other activities. Throughout the programme the 'I'm OK; you're OK' (Berne 1964) approach was adopted. This meant that everyone felt 'OK' about their 'self'. The programme also employed a peer-education approach that offered each young person opportunities to practise skills necessary for life and for continued recognition of respect for 'self' and others.

It is my intention to provide the adapted questionnaire developed over the years from the base of Maines and Robinson (1988) and the activities used as a standard part of the programme. There will be some references to alternative activities for specific settings or groups that have been developed since 1995. These activities are not just another set of photocopiable sheets, and do require some initial collecting together of artefacts. However, this is intentional, as the learners with whom I have worked and developed this programme have recognised the significance of 'real touchy-feely' resources, to quote one such learner.

Burns (1982) believes that some people need to be taught how to accept positive feedback. Lawrence (1973) described self-esteem as the difference between the perceived self-image and the ideal image. The self-image is that which is acquired and influenced by the individual's view of how they are accepted and valued by others. The ideal image is the individual's view of their desired abilities and qualities. The programme in 1989 appears to have assisted in the journey between the two for those young people who took part. It is my hope that many more young people can now begin that journey.

The *B/G Steem* Scales

Self-esteem Scale for Males 12 - 18 years

Self-esteem Scale for Females 12 - 18 years

Score Sheet for 12 - 18 years

Score Chart for Self-esteem Items

Score Chart for Locus of Control Items

B/G Steem Scales

I have adapted the original questionnaire and used it as a single page printed sheet of questions.

The programme outlined in this book focuses on 12-18 year olds.

Notes on administration of the scale

The form of the scale may be given on a group or individual basis. A computer version of the original Maines and Robinson questionnaire is available and can be used by one child at a time. The questions can be read to children if more appropriate. Question 2 offers an alternative for boys and girls. All question-naires should be answered by circling YES or NO.

If pupils do not live with their parent(s) then questions 6,12,18,24,31,34 (secondary) refer to the adults where they live.

Scoring the written form

A score sheet is provided that shows each question and indicates the response that will register a positive score. Locus of control items (seven on each scale) are identified by an asterisk. Two scores are obtained, one for the self-esteem items and one for the locus of control.

Compare the respondent's record with the score sheet and score '1' wherever the two match, counting the locus of control items separately.

Maximum scores (secondary)

28 self-esteem	7 locus of control

Record the two scores in the boxes and compare the respondent's scores with the table of norms using the appropriate column for age and gender. This will indicate whether the scores fall into the normal range or are unusually high or low.

Used as a tool for identification, alongside the exercises and activities, the questionnaire has provided a sound design to ensure development of confidence, aspiration and self-esteem.

The following quote is from a former group member who wishes to remain unnamed and who now works with young offenders.

> "It helped me see who I could be and then to become who I wanted to be. Thanks."

Self-esteem Scale For Males 12-18 years

Please answer by circling YES or NO

1	Is your school or college work good?	Yes No
2	Do you like being male?	Yes No
3	Are you strong and healthy?	Yes No
4	Does someone else always choose what you wear?	Yes No
5	Do you feel people get angry with you?	Yes No
6	Do your family think you behave well?	Yes No
7	Do others like socialising with you?	Yes No
8	Do you think you are nice looking?	Yes No
9	Are you as clever as others in your school or college?	Yes No
10	Do you worry a lot?	Yes No
11	Does the teacher notice when you work hard?	Yes No
12	Do your family make you feel silly?	Yes No
13	Are you sporty?	Yes No
14	Do others choose you to join in with them?	Yes No
15	Can you improve your work if you really try?	Yes No
16	Are you good at academic work?	Yes No
17	Are you good at looking after yourself?	Yes No
18	Do adults at home like you to help them?	Yes No
19	Do you think people like you?	Yes No
20	Do you worry about how you look?	Yes No
21	Do you have a best friend?	Yes No
22	Is your teacher or tutor ever pleased with your achievements?	Yes No
23	Do you need a lot of help?	Yes No
24	Are your family usually fair?	Yes No
25	If someone doesn't understand you can you explain what you want or need?	Yes No
26	Do you find maths hard?	Yes No
27	Do you have nice clothes?	Yes No
28	Are you bullied or picked on?	Yes No
29	Do you feel people have decided everything about your life for you?	Yes No
30	Are you one of the best looking in your group?	Yes No
31	Do you have a good relationship with someone at home?	Yes No
32	Do you make excuses for making lots of mistakes?	Yes No
33	Do you think that wishing may make nice things happen?	Yes No
34	Are your family cross with you for no reason?	Yes No
35	Do you often wish you were someone else?	Yes No

Thank you

Self-esteem Scale For Females 12-18 years

Please answer by circling YES or NO

1   Is your school or college work good? _____ Yes   No
2   Do you like being female? _____ Yes   No
3   Are you strong and healthy? _____ Yes   No
4   Does someone else always choose what you wear? _____ Yes   No
5   Do you feel people get angry with you? _____ Yes   No
6   Do your family think you behave well? _____ Yes   No
7   Do others like socialising with you? _____ Yes   No
8   Do you think you are nice looking? _____ Yes   No
9   Are you as clever as others in your school or college? _____ Yes   N
10 Do you worry a lot? _____ Yes   No
11 Does the teacher notice when you work hard? _____ Yes   No
12 Do your family make you feel silly? _____ Yes   No
13 Are you sporty? _____ Yes   No
14 Do others choose you to join in with them? _____ Yes   No
15 Can you improve your work if you really try? _____ Yes   No
16 Are you good at academic work? _____ Yes   No
17 Are you good at looking after yourself? _____ Yes   No
18 Do adults at home like you to help them? _____ Yes   No
19 Do you think people like you? _____ Yes   No
20 Do you worry about how you look? _____ Yes   No
21 Do you have a best friend? _____ Yes   No
22 Is your teacher or tutor ever pleased with your achievements? _____ Yes   No
23 Do you need a lot of help? _____ Yes   No
24 Are your family usually fair? _____ Yes   No
25 If someone doesn't understand you can you explain
    what you want or need? _____ Yes   No
26 Do you find maths hard? _____ Yes   No
27 Do you have nice clothes? _____ Yes   No
28 Are you bullied or picked on? _____ Yes   No
29 Do you feel people have decided everything about your life for you? Yes   No
30 Are you one of the best looking in your group? _____ Yes   No
31 Do you have a good relationship with someone at home? _____ Yes   No
32 Do you make excuses for making lots of mistakes? _____ Yes   No
33 Do you think that wishing may make nice things happen? _____ Yes   No
34 Are your family cross with you for no reason? _____ Yes   No
35 Do you often wish you were someone else? _____ Yes   No

Thank you

Score sheet for 12-18 years

A 1	Is your school or college work good?	_____	Yes
G 2	Do you like being male/female?	_____	Yes
P 3	Are you strong and healthy?	_____	Yes
L 4	Does someone else always choose what you wear?	_____	*No
G 5	Do you feel people get angry with you?	_____	No
F 6	Do your family think you behave well?	_____	Yes
S 7	Do others like socialising with you?	_____	Yes
P 8	Do you think you are nice looking?	_____	Yes
A 9	Are you as clever as others in your school or college?	_____	Yes
G 10	Do you worry a lot?	_____	No
L 11	Does the teacher notice when you work hard?	_____	*Yes
F 12	Do your family make you feel silly?	_____	No
P 13	Are you sporty?	_____	Yes
S 14	Do others choose you to join in with them?	_____	Yes
L 15	Can you improve your work if you really try?	_____	*Yes
A 16	Are you good at academic work?	_____	Yes
G 17	Are you good at looking after yourself?	_____	Yes
F 18	Do adults at home like you to help them?	_____	Yes
L 19	Do you think people like you?	_____	*Yes
P 20	Do you worry about how you look?	_____	No
S 21	Do you have a best friend?	_____	Yes
A 22	Is your teacher or tutor ever pleased with your achievements?	_____	Yes
G 23	Do you need a lot of help?	_____	No
F 24	Are your family usually fair?	_____	Yes
L 25	If someone doesn't understand you can you explain what you want or need?	_____	*Yes
A 26	Do you find maths hard?	_____	No
P 27	Do you have nice clothes?	_____	Yes
S 28	Are you bullied or picked on?	_____	No
L 29	Do you feel people have decided everything about your life for you?	_____	*No
P 30	Are you one of the best looking in your group?	_____	Yes
F 31	Do you have a good relationship with someone at home?	_____	Yes
A 32	Do you make excuses for making lots of mistakes?	_____	No
L 33	Do you think that wishing may make nice things happen?	_____	*Yes
F 34	Are your family cross with you for no reason?	_____	No
G 35	Do you often wish you were someone else?	_____	No

Asterisk scores are locus of control items

Score charts

Males

Age	Very Low	Low	Normal	High	Very High
6-8 yrs	Less than 12	12-14	15-17	18	19-20
9-11 yrs	Less than 12	12-13	14-16	17-18	19-20
12-18 yrs	Less than 17	17-18	19-22	23-24	25-28

Females

Age	Very Low	Low	Normal	High	Very High
6-8 yrs	Less than 12	12-13	14-17	18	19-20
9-11 yrs	Less than 11	11-13	14-17	18	19-20
12-18 yrs	Less than 14	14-18	19-21	22-24	25-28

Score Chart For Locus Of Control Items

Males

Age	External	Normal	Internal
6-8 yrs	0-2	3-4	5-7
9-11 yrs	0-3	4-5	6-7
12-18 yrs	0-5	6	7

Females

Age	External	Normal	Internal
6-8 yrs	0-2	3-4	5-7
9-11 yrs	0-4	5	6-7
12-18 yrs	0-5	6	7

The questions were distributed in the seven categories as follows:

General=6 Social=4 Academic=6 Physical=4
Family=6 Lie=4 Locus of Control=10
Total=40

Using this Programme

This pack and its activities are meant to support and give ideas. It is not intended to either be used in isolation from other activities or without consideration of the individual needs, skills or experiences of those involved. It is expected that the facilitator will have some experience in working with groups, and will incorporate these activities into an established or familiar way of working with young people who have difficulties with feelings of self-worth. The facilitator will know his or her target group and I recommend a minimum of ten hours with a selection of exercises from each of the sections.

Opening Session

This session is set out as a welcoming and assessment session and should always be used to start working with the group for the first time.

'Introductory', 'Moving On' and 'Closing' Activities

During the duration of the programme, usually about ten weeks, it is recommended that the facilitator uses an appropriate selection of activities from each of these sections, according to the development and needs of the group.

The duration of the programme and the number of sessions is not prescribed – I used activities with young offenders as a programme of three hours per week over ten weeks and as an inclusion programme over six weeks.

It is important that people do not see this programme as just a 'topic' similar to drugs or diet or hygiene. It is equally important that they do not see a healthy lifestyle as 'don't do…' or 'give up…' In order to avoid this, the following points need to be remembered:

- People with low self-esteem find it difficult to try new things.

- Know the activity or resource you are using.

- Get back-up leaflets, speakers or other similar inputs if you feel it is necessary.

- Maintain a holistic or whole-person approach.

- Do not forget that the child or young person has experience too.

- Go for a balance of delivery styles.

- Make sure positive feedback is given wherever possible.

- Ensure equality of opportunity in the style of your delivery.

- It is OK not to know the answer.

Use the skills of any local peer educators who can offer support. I always encourage those who have been through the process to assist with the delivery to future groups; this helps to continue their own learning and accreditation opportunities while reinforcing their positive self-esteem.

Peer education is sometimes difficult for adults to accept or allow. It means letting go of the control or power and allowing young people to lead the way. Obvious safety precautions need to be considered, but the easiest way to ensure this is to share the policies of the institution or organisation, draw up ground rules and work within those jointly created boundaries.

Objectives

- to give children and young people the opportunity to be involved in a safe learning environment

- to enable children and young people to recognise their true 'self' and feel OK with it

- to provide a structure to practise and develop skills of positive thinking and behaviour

- to support the growth of empathy

- to support the development of reflection

- to recognise how others see us

- to discuss and prioritise appropriate coping strategies for different situations

- to provide a group support framework in order to move forwards

- to increase confidence and internal motivation

- to provide a focus in the form of a project to encourage achievement that will have a lasting effect on other curriculum areas and throughout life.

The diagram 'The Stages that Empower People' on page 20 illustrates how the development of the group is experienced by the individuals as the objectives are achieved. This page could be used as part of the final review during the last session.

The Planning Wheel

If the programme is to:

- run smoothly

- enlist the support of colleagues

- achieve demonstrable results

then the plan below will be useful. It is well worth spending some time in preparation before commencing work with young people.

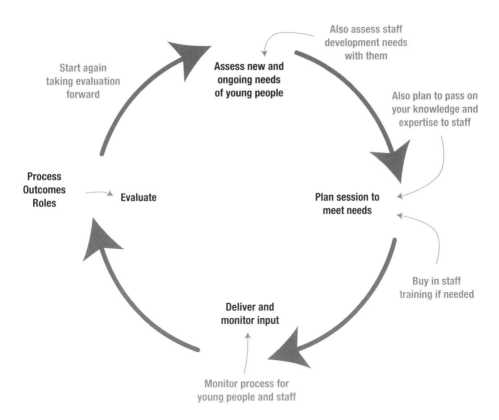

The Stages That Empower People

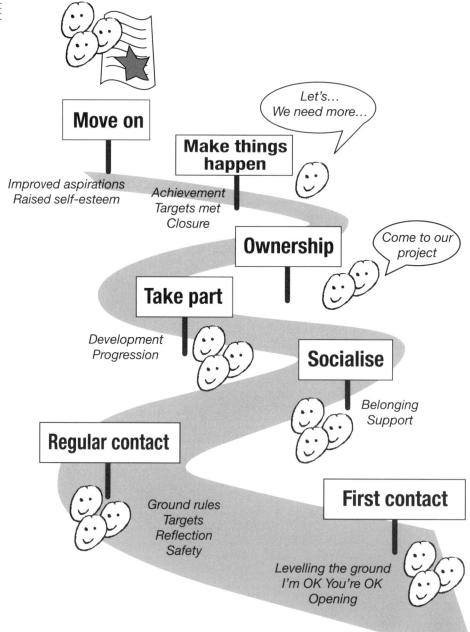

Opening Session

Opening session

Aim

- to encourage each young person to feel valued
- to establish some sense of belonging
- to measure self-esteem at this stage.

Objectives

Each young person will:

- complete a self esteem measure
- identify what influences their behaviours and lifestyle
- explore what worries them
- set targets.

This opening session is the only set session until the final session. This foundation is crucial and I have found this format to be very successful with all the groups that have used it. When I have not followed this format the programmes have been less successful.

Welcome and ground levelling

You will know your group and why they are with you. It is important that this learning process is not seen as a punishment, nor as a treat and that a clean slate is the starting point. Open the group by:

- welcoming participants
- explaining the purpose of the meetings
- using the Ground Rules sheet to establish the way you will work to-gether.

Present

I always give a 'present' to each member. This is based on my previous knowledge of the individuals and is totally altruistic in that I believe everyone should have the right to the feeling of being valued. It is also true that the individuals who attend this programme may not easily receive any positive input from any other significant adult. These 'presents' could be:

- a sandwich (if it is lunch-time)
- a drink
- a copy of a poem I have used to begin the session
- a map

- playing a piece of music.

It is important to let the group know why you are giving the present; it is because you wanted to! It is not a bribe, it is a genuine gift you wanted to share with them.

Self-esteem measure

- Give a brief introduction to show that you empathise with some of the difficulties that are being experienced.

- Distribute the Cooley's Looking Glass Theory handout. We learn to know who we are from the messages we receive from others – it works like a mirror. If we are praised and celebrated then we are more likely to accept this and develop a positive self-image. If we are rejected and criticised then we lose confidence and feel bad about ourselves.

- Discuss with the group members how their identified difficulties might be explained by this theory. Explain that over the course of this programme support mechanisms and structures will be put in place to improve the situation.

- Distribute and complete the self-esteem measure sheets found on pages 10-11. These can be scored by the facilitator at any time.

Team building

Ask the group to do the Chart Topping exercise and discuss their choices. Then move the discussion on to a reflection on how the group members worked during this activity. Use the Team Building sheet to facilitate the discussion. The development of the team depends upon each individual demonstrating the elements in the handout. You should encourage participants to assess their own skills for each element. Positive feedback and immediate reward is the key here.

Finally

Ask everybody to say how they found today's session and set one target as a group on this occasion:

"Be here next time and enjoy the next session."

Before the next session select which activities from each section to use. I suggest one per session to leave room for target setting.

Ground Rules

I agree to stick to the following ground rules:

1. Turn up on time and if I can't, let...know.

2. Respect! Myself; my group; my meeting space.

3. Be honest! If I'm struggling, my group can help.

4. Enjoy!

Signed .... Preferred name ....

Cooley's Looking Glass Theory

Chart Topping

You will need:

- Copies of the Chart Topping handout.

What now?

- Ask the young people to chart the top sounds that they feel represent their lives.
- The facilitator might offer an example from his or her adolescence.
- Discuss.
- Possibly decide on a focus for further work.

Chart Topping

Team Building

How do you rate yourself for each of the skills? Circle the number beside each word, 0 being poor and 10 being excellent.

Communication

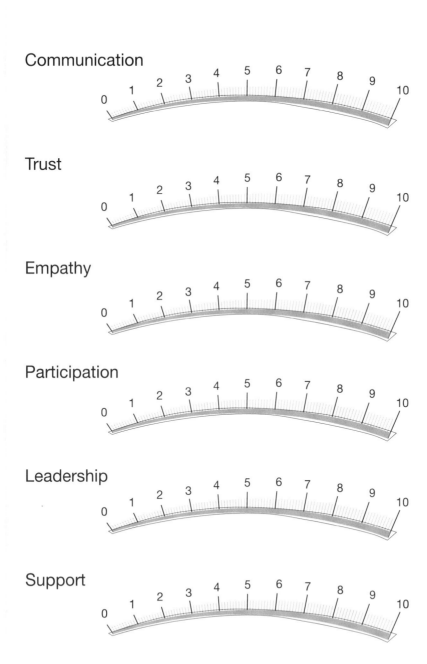

Trust

Empathy

Participation

Leadership

Support

Opening Activities

What Affects Your Lifestyle?

This has been successful in school assemblies, on a field with detached work and as a trigger session in a group in order to focus.

You will need:

- a suitcase
- a collection of tapes, money, magazines, posters, empty tablet containers, alcohol bottles, cans, map, mirror, make-up, condoms and anything you think has an effect on the health choices of young people (be creative).

What now?

- Ask the young people to select something that they feel affects them and their choices and discuss as a group.

- If you identify a common issue you can then focus on that issue for some further work or agree targets around it.

Hang Out Your Worries

You will need:

- a length of washing line
- paper or card
- clothes pegs
- pens.

What now?

- You need to erect a 'washing line' and have paper or card and pegs to hand.

- Ask each young person to record one or two 'worries' that they have and peg them on the line.

- Discuss one-to-one or in a group and set targets to overcome or improve the 'worry'.

- Alternatively you could use the worries below and ask the young people to peg them in rank of concern along the line and discuss.
  I've got no friends.
  I'm too fat.
  My trainers are rubbish and so on.

Expectations Ladder

Designed to identify the distance between self and ideal self. This results in being able to set realistic expectations and achievable targets.

You will need:

- pens
- A2 paper.

What now?

- Draw a ladder or ask the young person to do so. Also draw the young person (or have a photo).

- Ask the young person to place themselves on a rung of the ladder and note their current strengths below that rung.

- Ask the young person to identify what they would like to achieve, be like, have and so on at the top and to break down what is in between the current position and aspired.

- Discuss, set targets, note possible future strategies and support. It may be useful to identify what led to these strengths or achievements.

Inside Out

This is a trigger exercise to encourage the young person to begin to accept responsibility for their behaviour and learning (one-to-one or small group).

You will need:

- pen
- Inside Out Statement Cards on the handout
- A2 paper.

What now?

- Copy the Inside Out Statements sheet and cut out each card. There is also a blank sheet for you to provide your own statements.

- On the A2 paper, write 'Me' on the left hand side of the paper and 'Others' on the right hand side.

- Discuss the statements and ask the young person to place them where they think they should go: either under the 'me' or 'others' statement. The 'me' are those things within our control – internal. The 'others' are those influences less easy to control or change – external.

- Discuss and set targets.

Inside Out Statements

My bedroom is messy because I have lots of stuff.	My hair is horrible because I have to wear hairgrips.
My clothes are nice because I choose them.	The teachers don't like me because I'm not clever.
I'm often getting told off for forgetting my workbook.	I do well with my work because I concentrate.
I am rubbish at maths because it is too hard.	I get told off at home because they won't let me play on the computer.

Inside Out Statements

Sign Posts

You will need:

- the Risk Statement handout.
- A2 paper and pen.

What now?

- Divide a large sheet of paper into three columns and label each one either:

  Traffic Lights = Definitely OK! Low risk.
  Give Way = Think about it! Medium risk.
  No Entry = Definitely not! High risk.

- Ask the young people to take a statement, read it out and place it where they think it best fits regarding the risk factor.

- Ask for further suggestions for risk factor cards as well as those we have provided.

Risk Statements

Having a drink and driving.	Not doing homework.
Riding a bike with no helmet.	Saying 'no' to drugs.
Bunking off school or work.	Using drugs.
Kicking off at school or college.	Joy-riding.
Being alone all the time.	Fighting.
Having no friends.	Bullying.
Going out with more than one partner at the same time.	Messing around at work.
Kissing.	Doing something illegal.

I Know What You Know I Know

You will need:

- the I Know What You Know I Know worksheet.

What next?

This needs to be used twice throughout the course of the programme to help show progression of self and group work: once after the opening activities and again as part of the closing activities. It assists self-exploration: the 'me' inside and the 'me' revealed to others. It works well used alongside 'Mirror, Mirror' and 'Inside Out'. The activity can be used as a group exercise but members can choose to disclose or withhold their answers to list three.

I Know What You Know I Know

LIST 1
What you and others know
about you.

_____

_____

_____

_____

LIST 2
What others know about you
of which you're unsure (usually
given by feedback, for example,
mannerisms).

_____

_____

_____

_____

LIST 3
What you know but choose to
keep hidden from others.

_____

_____

_____

_____

LIST 4
What you don't know and
others don't know (because you
haven't tried it yet).

_____

_____

_____

_____

Moving On Activities

Me Tree

You will need:

- Me Tree handouts, 1 and 2.

What now?

- Using the Me Tree 1 handout, ask the young person to write each letter of their name in the tree making sure there is room to write after each letter. Discuss and record in the branches how the young person sees themselves, using each letter to start the word. (for example, A.N.N.E. becomes Anxious, Naughty, Nice, Energetic.)

- Discuss and record on the trunk things that influence this image and consequent behaviour.

- Discuss and record in the roots no more than five things that the young person thinks have been positive aspects of home, school and social life to date.

- Discuss and circle aspects of the branch or trunk that can be set as a target for improvement for Me Tree 2 and write the date of your next Me Tree meeting.

Example:

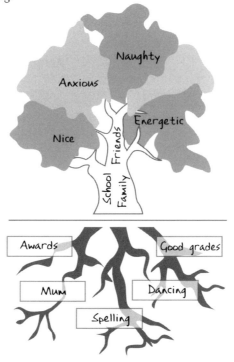

Me Tree 1

Name...Date ....

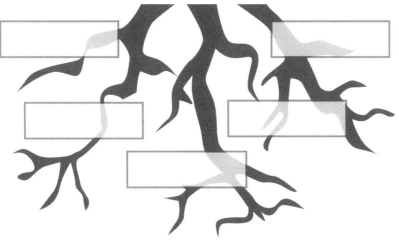

Me Tree 2

Name..Date ....

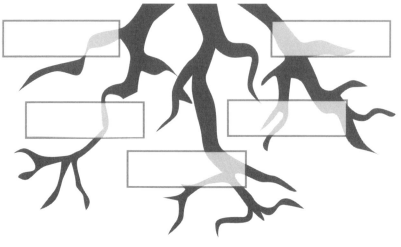

What Does It For You?

You will need:

- a copy of the handout What Does It For You?
- some method of recording the discussion (flip chart, video, audio tape).

What now?

- Explain what A B C stands for in terms of behaviour:

  A – Antecedent – what happens to trigger the reaction?

  B – Behaviour – ways you have responded to the trigger
     (the antecedent).

  C – Consequences – what happened because of your response?

- After each person has given an example discuss alternative responses and strategies for coping. Set targets.

What Does It For You?

Sometimes the way we react to different situations may lead to us feeling upset. Think of something that has made you feel sad, angry or upset and make a note of it to discuss in your group.

Antecedent

Behaviour

Consequences

Me And My Group

You will need:

- a body outline (large size – life-size is excellent)
- pens, paint or similar.

What now?

- Ask the young people, either individually or in groups, to write or draw what they are made up of, and about their health and wellbeing in the body shape. Here is an example:

- In pairs allow them to discuss differences and similarities and feed back to the whole group.

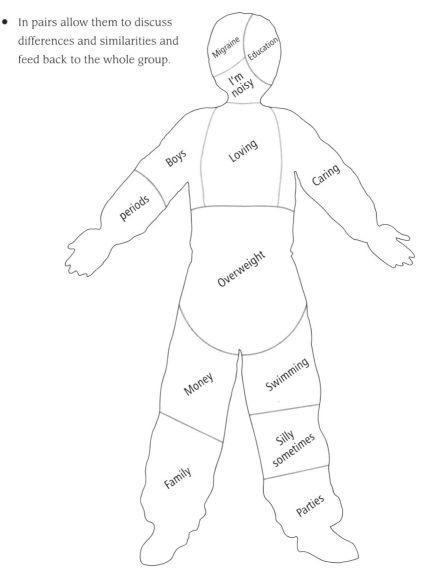

Diamond Nine Feelings

You will need:

- Nine cards or Post-Its.

What now?

- Ask the young person to write, draw or record a feeling or incident either positive or negative on each of the nine cards or Post-Its.

- Discuss and ask the young person to prioritise these feelings;

  1 = most important to them

  9 = least important

  4, 5 and 6 can be equal.

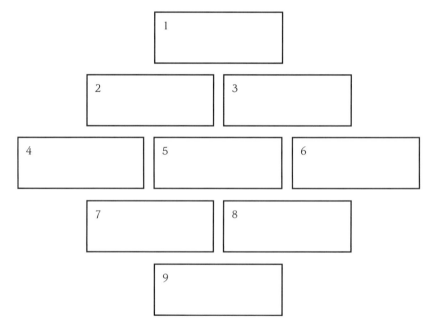

- One-to-one or in a small group discuss the antecedent to these feelings and set targets for change.

Sunshine of Success

You will need:

- Copies of the Sunshine of Success handout

What now?

- As a group or one-to-one, discuss and record on the sun's rays what will make the sun smile. Fill in the targets in the boxes.

- When the recorded targets are met add a smile to the sun's face. (Simple but effective.)

Completing every homework.

Going to bed before midnight every night.

Turning up on time for a week.

Feeling better about my body.

Making the most of my time in school.

Helping my little sister with her work.

Sunshine of Success

Mirror, Mirror

You will need:

- A mirror that can be passed around.

What now?

- Sit in a circle or around a table and ask each young person to look into the mirror and say something positive about themselves.

- The rest of the group say 'mirror mirror' if they agree with the statement and 'mirror' if they don't. If they don't, the person has another go.

- Pass the mirror on and repeat until all members have had three goes.

It is important to explain before starting that when saying their positive statements, 'always' and 'never' are not allowed – only 'sometimes'! This illuminates 'I'm always naughty' and so on.

This has been most successful when the adult joins in and has been exciting done against the clock.

Warning: It is important that, by the time this activity is used, the group is working well and members can be relied upon to support each other. Do not risk the activity if it might cause hurt to vulnerable members of the group.

Another Brick in The Wall

This exercise is designed to highlight the importance of everyone; each individual has a strength that makes the group, class, whole world better!

You will need:

- A4 paper or boxes if you intend a 3D result
- pens.

What now?

- Ask the young people to work in pairs to discuss their strengths.

- Each young person records their strengths on the papers or boxes.

- The whole group build the wall and discuss the strengths, the group and how it could be even stronger.

- Set targets.

- The wall can be added to if the programme is long term so that group members can 'see' their success.

What? Me?

You will need:

- The Positive and Negative Statements sheets.

What now?

- Ask each of the young people to pick a positive and a negative statement (this is down to individual interpretation and must not be challenged).

- In pairs discuss why these were chosen.

- Work in larger groups to discuss where these messages came from to give individuals their feelings: media, society, family and similar.

- Decide how to move forward. For example, write to advertisers, speak to the family, design a counter-balance poster.

- This activity also works well with enlarged statements placed on the ground for discussion. Symbols and pictures have also proved useful.

Positive Statements

I like my hair when it's just been washed.	I am working hard to meet my targets.
I'm a good shape to cuddle.	I'm happy with my body shape.
I'm clever.	I look good in shorts.
I'm quite clever.	I have nice coloured eyes.
My legs are really strong, I can walk for miles.	I have a loving family.
I've got a muscular body.	I like the way I look after a hard workout.
My body is strong and supple.	I challenge bullies.
I enjoy pampering my body.	I enjoy dancing.
I support my friends.	I walk gracefully.
I have my own sort of style.	I am easy to talk to.

Negative Statements

I hate my bum in trousers.	My body is a total mess.
Keeners make me sick.	I look much better when I've got make-up on.
I only feel handsome when people pay me compliments.	There's no point in trying at school.
I look better in baggy clothes.	I'm going to drop out as soon as I'm 16.
My life will be better when I leave school, college or home.	I give people as good as I get.
I'm too embarrassed to go to the gym.	At my age there's no point making an effort with my appearance.
It's a good job I'm tall, it means I don't look as fat.	My family nags me all the time.
My body is wimpish.	Nobody likes me.
I'm useless at everything.	I'm never going to amount to anything.
I'll never find someone who loves me.	People don't understand me.

Closing Activities

Relationship Tree

This discussion 'trigger' game has been a hit with various groups in many different settings.

You will need:

- the Relationship Tree handouts or
- paper to draw a tree on.

What now?

1) Draw a tree or use the one on the handout.

2) Discuss the 'roots' of a positive relationship and the outcomes (leaves can 'grow' to show the next stage of the relationship).

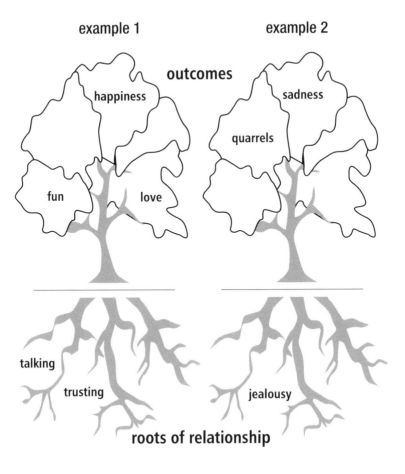

example 1   example 2

outcomes

happiness   sadness

quarrels

fun   love

talking

trusting   jealousy

roots of relationship

Relationship Tree

Stressed Out?

This activity acknowledges that everyone feels stressed at times. It's a levelling activity to ensure individuals feel OK about this. It looks at ways of responding to that stress and gives a perfect lead into discussion and setting targets to respond appropriately in different situations.

You will need:

- Stressed Out? worksheet

What now?

- Individuals complete the Stressed Out? worksheet.

- Share and discuss in the group.

- Set targets to change any behaviours identified as inappropriate (one at a time may be suitable for some members of the group).

- This exercise can also be played like a game of bingo to help the individual identify his or her behaviour. Pictures to assist can also be used.

Stressed Out?

Everyone gets stressed at some time in their day. Circle your stress and reactions then talk with a mate in the group.

Situation	Noisy response	Quiet response
Missing a bus	Swearing	Looking for the time of the next bus
Being told off for something you have done wrong in class	Shouting	a) apologising b) block it out
Being told off for something you have not done wrong in class	Shouting	a) explain the truth b) see teacher after class and explain
Someone picking on you	Hitting out	Hiding
Someone calling you names	Picking a fight	Pretend you didn't hear
Parents/carers asking about your day	Arguing	Discussing
Being criticised about your work or achievement	Destroying the work or certificate	Not bothering to achieve

Put Up Your Umbrella

This exercise raises the discussion of pressures surrounding young people when making choices.

You will need:

- Put Up Your Umbrella handout
- Raindrops handout
- paper and glue
- or an umbrella and Post-Its.

What now?

- Give the young people the Raindrops Sheet and the Put Up Your Umbrella sheet. Find a way to enlarge the images.

  If using a real umbrella use Post-Its or if using the printed activity sheet use the paper cut out raindrops, and ask the young people to write or draw things that:

  - confuse them (unsure items)
  - contradict what they think or know (unsure items)
  - assist them and make them more certain in making choices (sure items).

- Either paste on to the paper sheet or stick on to the umbrella surfaces

  - above the shelter the unsure items
  - below the shelter the sure items

  as if being sheltered from the 'rain of uncertainty'.

- Discuss.

Put Up Your Umbrella

Raindrops

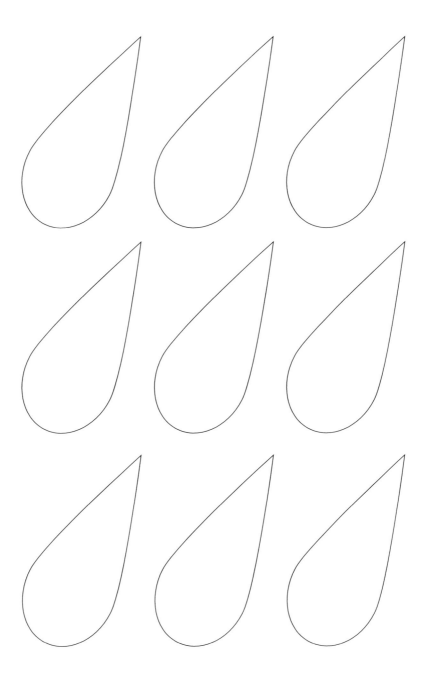

Okay Relationships

These can be difficult to discuss but here's a game that might help.

You will need:

- Acceptable or Unacceptable Statement Cards
- a group of people.

What now?

- Share out the cards.

- Have one end of paper, table or other area as 'acceptable' and the opposite end as 'unacceptable'.

- People place their card in the place they think it belongs.

  Cards will be at various positions:

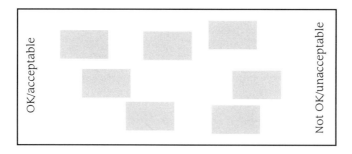

- To move a card the whole group needs to negotiate.

This can be fun and may promote a lot of discussion.

If you want to continue at a later time then just blu-tac cards onto a large sheet of paper to save.

Try asking the group to turn the statements into positives so that all the group members reach a consensus of agreement that they are acceptable.

Acceptable Or Unacceptable Statement cards

Not listening to people.	People not listening to you.
Being late for a class, a date or an appointment.	Calling someone a slag.
Being called a slag.	Showing off.
Saying sorry.	Admitting you like somebody
Being individual.	Crying.
Helping.	Sharing friends.
Achieving.	Being two-faced.

Friendship Circle

You will need:

- A group of people.

What now?

- Ask the group to stand in a circle.

- Each young person needs to pay a compliment of some description to the person on their left, and only when this is done can that person hold hands (this works like a chain reaction).

- When the circle is complete sit down and discuss the process and the need to try to be nice to others, even though sometimes it's hard.

- Set any targets identified.

With an individual

- Ask the young person to identify who are their friends and say something positive about each one.

- Ask the young person to identify those they have problems with but to say something positive about each one.

- When the circle is complete sit down and discuss the process, and the need to try to be nice to others even though sometimes it's hard.

- Set any targets identified.

I Know What You Know I Know

You will need:

- the I Know What You Know I Know worksheet.

What next?

You should have completed this exercise earlier in the programme. Ask the group to complete the sheet again, noting the differences.

I Know What You Know I Know (Reprise)

LIST 1
What you and others know
about you.

_____

_____

_____

_____

LIST 2
What others know about you
of which you're unsure (usually
given by feedback, for example,
mannerisms).

_____

_____

_____

_____

LIST 3
What you know but choose to
keep hidden from others.

_____

_____

_____

_____

LIST 4
What you don't know and
others don't know (because you
haven't tried it yet).

_____

_____

_____

_____

Appendix

Certificates – Celebration of Course Completion

Evaluation

Celebration
of
Course Completion

This is to certify that

_____

has been brilliant because:

_____

_____

_____

_____

Signed _____   Signed _____

Date _____   Date _____

Celebration of Course Completion

This is to certify that

_____

has met the necessary negotiated agreed targets:

_____

_____

_____

_____

Signed _____   Signed _____

Date _____   Date _____

Evaluation

You have been great! Please tell me how you have found these sessions by rating each statement out of four in the relevant box.
1 = don't agree 4 = strongly agree

I feel good about myself ☐

I don't feel any different about myself ☐

I enjoyed this group ☐

I learned a lot ☐

I did well ☐

The activities were cool ☐

Other people know I did well ☐

School has improved ☐

Home has improved ☐

Bibliography

Berne, E. (1964) *Games People Play.* Penguin.

Biggs, J.B. (1978) 'Individual and group differences in study processes'. *British Journal of Educational Psychology* 48: pp 266-279.

Biggs & Kirby (1984) Mediational approach to learning and study processes, *British Journal Educational Psychology.*

Burns, R. (1982) *Self-concept, development and education.* Hoff, Rinehart & Winston.

Cooley, C.H. (1922) *Human Nature and the Social Order.* Charles Scribner's Sons.

Harvey, M. (2000) Relationships between adolescents' attachment styles and family functioning, *Adolescence.*

Lawrence, D. (1973) *Improved reading through counselling.* Ward Lock.

Maines, B. & Robinson, G. (1988) *B/G Steem; A self-esteem scale with locus of control items.* Lucky Duck Publishing.

Maslow, H. A. (1968) *Toward a Psychology of Being.* D. Van Nostrand Co.

Nelson-Jones, R. (1993) *Practical Counselling and Helping Skills: how to use the life skills helping mode.* Cassel.

Plutchik, R. (1962) *The Emotions: facts, theories and a new model.* Random House.

Tomlinson, N. (2004) Report 14-19 Curriculum and Qualifications Reform.